BEN NUTTALL'S
FOOTY FACTORY

Thank you to my family and partner for always supporting me, my brother Luke for helping me film (no matter the weather!) for over a decade, and all of the amazing readers who watch my content.

Make sure you talk to a trusted grown-up before you search for anything online. This includes skills, famous footy moments, or when you're using the QR code in this book.

With thanks to Rebaz Mohammed, Jake Hope, and William Brickell and Philip Broom of Brighton and Hove Albion FC Foundation

Ben Nuttall's Footy Factory is a Fox & Ink Books book

First published in Great Britain in 2026 by
Fox & Ink Books
The University of Lancashire
Preston, PR1 2HE, UK

Text copyright © Emma Roberts, 2026
Illustrations © Nigel Baines, 2026
Additional images © Adobe Stock, 2026

978-1-917894-06-7

1 3 5 7 9 10 8 6 4 2

Design by Amy Cooper.

A CIP catalogue record for this book is available from the British Library.
Printed and bound by L&C Printing Group, Poland.

MIX
Paper | Supporting responsible forestry
FSC® C152082

BEN NUTTALL'S

FOOTY FACTORY

by Ben Nuttall

with Emma Roberts

Illustrated by Nigel Baines

Fox & Ink Books

CONTENTS

p46 # IMPROVER SKILLS

p78   PRO SKILLS

Hi Team,

Welcome to Footy Factory – a world of tricks, challenges and footy fun!

In this book, you'll find skills of different levels, ready for wherever you're at on your football journey. Remember – everyone starts as a beginner when it comes to learning new tricks . . . me included. It's all about practice and dedication, but also, FUN!

Since I was a teenager, I've been travelling the world making my videos and showcasing my skills, as well as breaking world records and filming with the world's biggest football stars. BUT, I've also spent thousands of hours practising, and that'll never stop – there's still a whole kitbag full of footy stuff I want to do! I wonder what adventures football might bring YOU, if you work hard and dream big?

Right. Ready to top up your tekkers, supersize your skills AND have a laugh?
Let's kick off!

Ben

Marcelo

I love making videos, so I've made some EXCLUSIVE content, just for you! Ask an adult to help you scan the QR code wherever you find it in the book, to see me demonstrating each of the skills and lots more cool stuff!

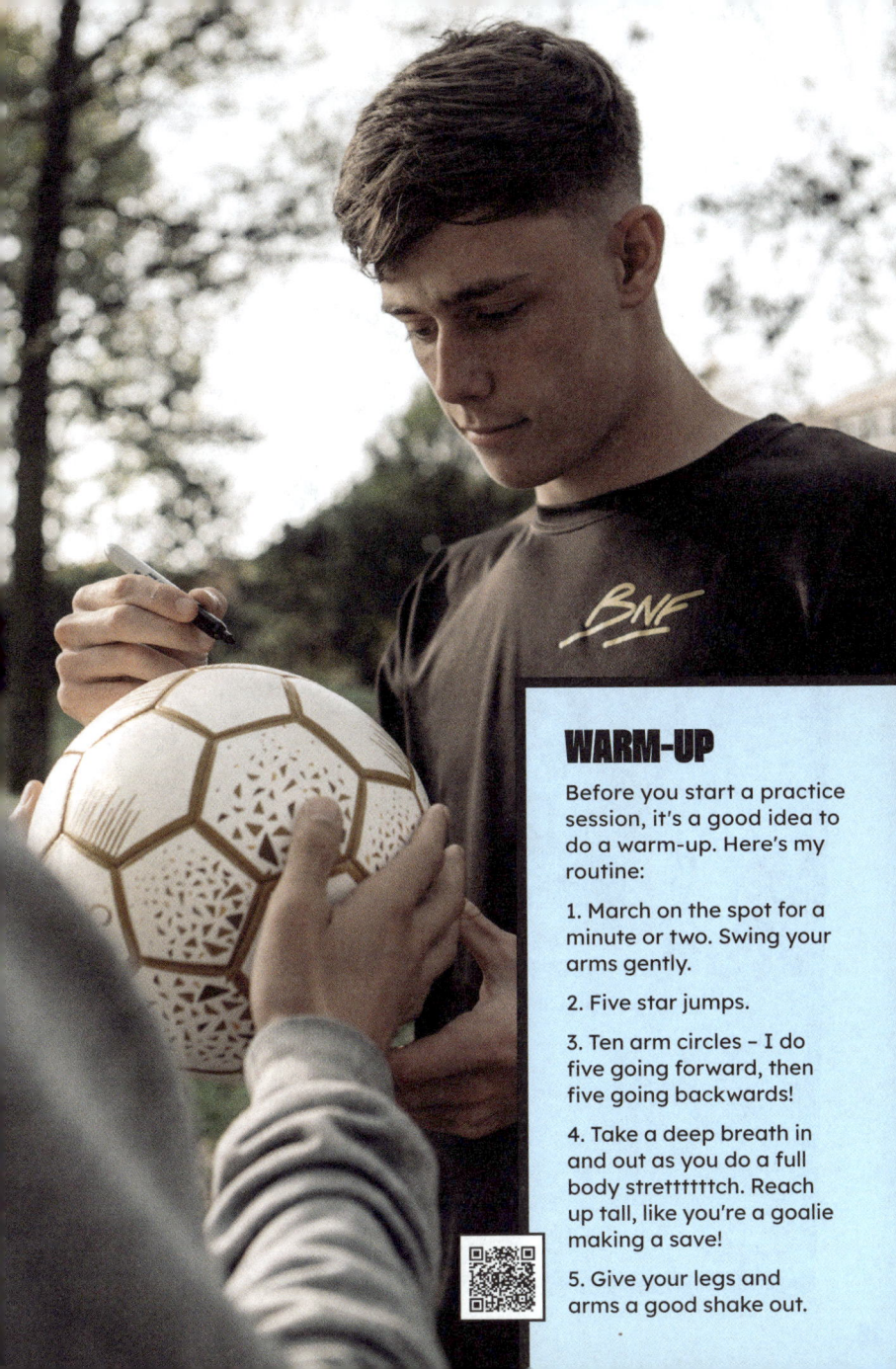

WARM-UP

Before you start a practice session, it's a good idea to do a warm-up. Here's my routine:

1. March on the spot for a minute or two. Swing your arms gently.

2. Five star jumps.

3. Ten arm circles – I do five going forward, then five going backwards!

4. Take a deep breath in and out as you do a full body stretttttttch. Reach up tall, like you're a goalie making a save!

5. Give your legs and arms a good shake out.

ROOKIE

HOW TO DRIBBLE

I promise our first skill has nothing to do with baby drool! In football, dribbling is about staying in control of the ball while moving it around the pitch. Try these drills to help you get confident.

1

Put the ball between your feet. Hop from one foot to the other as you use the inside of each foot to tap the ball back and forth. Keep a gentle bend in your knees.

Can you manage four taps in a row? How about ten?

Now try one tap with the outside of your foot, followed by one tap with the inside of the same foot.

Repeat on the other foot. Keep repeating!

2

3

Now, let's travel. Use the top of your foot (where the laces are) to tap the ball a little ahead of you. Take a step on your other foot to catch up with the ball, then tap it again with the first foot.

Speed up a bit and repeat the step-tap-step-tap rhythm.

Now try a few step-taps followed by one tap with your outside foot. That'll change the ball's direction.

More step-taps to move the ball forward, then chuck in a tap with your inside foot to change direction again. Nice!

4

EXTRA-TIME CHALLENGE

Now try Step 3 without looking at your feet. Try to keep the ball moving and under control while you keep your eyes peeled for teammates to pass to, or defenders coming in to try and take the ball!

Remember – just *TAP* the ball gently when you're dribbling, don't *KICK* it! You don't want to send it too far away, otherwise your opponent might sneak into the gap and steal it from you!

HOW TO JUGGLE

Don't worry – you don't have to be a clown to be a good juggler! Juggling the ball with your feet is a must-have skill for linking footy freestyle tricks together. Practise every day if you can!

1 Drop the ball in front of you. Before it hits the ground, stick your foot underneath and tap the ball back up to catch it in your hands.

Try on the other foot.

Make sure your toes are relaxed and pointing forwards.

Try to let the ball come towards your foot rather than lifting your foot up to the ball.

2

Now do the drop and tap- up but instead of a catch, let the ball bounce once.

Before it hits the ground again after the bounce, stick your other foot under the ball to tap it up.

Practise tap-up then bounce on one foot, tap-up then bounce on the other foot. Repeat as many times as you can.

3

When you're confident, lose the bounce. Tap the ball up with one foot, then as it's coming back down to the ground, tap it back up with your other foot, and repeat.

You're juggling! 👏

FREESTYLER FUN STUFF

Can you guess the world record for the number of juggles in one hour with alternating feet? Tang Jinfan from China was only ten years old when he smashed it!

75

660

8147

Answer on p125!

PULLBACK FLICK

Flick-up tricks like this one are great for building your confidence in moving the ball around. If you get this one smooth, you'll look like you've been doing freestyle for years!

1

Place the ball on the ground in front of you and put the sole of your strong foot on top. Your weak foot will be a bit behind.

2

Roll the ball back towards your weak foot with your strong foot.

18

3 Just as the ball touches the toes of your weak foot, jump off that foot. At the same time, scoop up the ball with the weak toes and lift your leg a bit. The momentum of lifting your leg will help you flick the ball up into the air.

4 You can be super chill and just catch the ball with your hands, or catch it with your strong foot and go straight into some juggling. Either way, you'll look cool!

Most footballers have a strong foot and a weak foot. If you're not sure which is which for you, try this quick test . . .

Stand at the bottom of some stairs and have a mate shout 'Go!'. Which foot takes the first step up the stairs? That's your strong foot!

ROOKIE

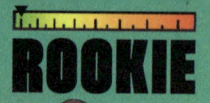

ROCKET LAUNCHER

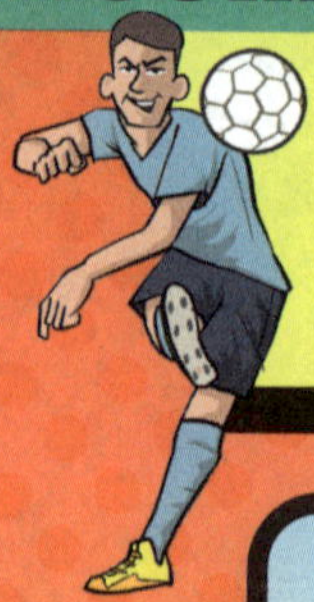

Ready to blast off to Planet Footy?! Here's a freestyle move that'll have you shooting for the moon!

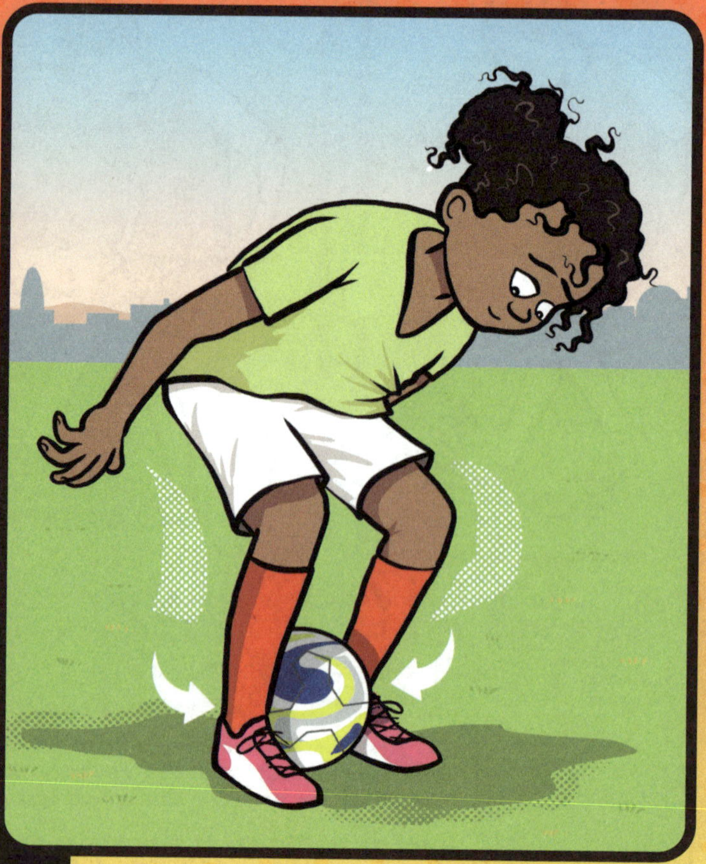

1 Squeeze the ball between your ankles. Squat down, keeping that ball trapped tight.

ROOKIE

2 Explode up into a jump, lifting your knees and releasing the squeeze on the ball as you go! The ball will shoot into the air with you.

3 Catch the ball with your hands.

> The deeper you squat, the higher you'll be able to drive yourself AND the ball up into the air!

FOOT STALL

This trick is all about beating the wobbles. You can build up slowly from the first step, and then add more difficulty once you get confident with your balance!

1 Place the ball in the space between your laces and the low part of your shin. Lift your toes a bit to help hold it there. Practise standing on one leg and balancing the ball in this position, then swap legs.

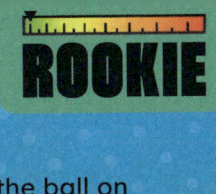
With the ball on the ground, try rolling it back with the sole of your foot then scooping it up into the Step 1 position with the same foot.

How's your balance? Keep working on it!

Roll back 👣

EXTRA-TIME CHALLENGE

Drop the ball from waist height and catch it on the top of your toes (not your laces, or it'll bounce away). Then show off your balancing skills!

Try to let your foot move WITH the ball as it lands on your toes, by gently lowering it. That's called 'cushioning'. Make sure your foot is relaxed too. The ball will BOING right off a rigid foot!

ROOKIE

RONALDO CHOP

Want to play like Cristiano Ronaldo? Nail this move he invented, and you're guaranteed to catch any defender off guard!

1 Start off by dribbling the ball. When you're ready for the trick, the next time you land your weak foot on the ground, do a little hop off of it.

Weak foot

2 Lift your strong leg up and a little to the side as you hop, then quickly bring the inside of the strong foot to the outside of the ball.

Use the inside of the foot to send the ball sideways, behind your weak leg. That's the chop. Then plant your weak foot into the ground. Try and plant it so your toes are pointing in the direction of the ball.

Quickly turn your whole body in that direction and follow the ball, leaving the defender scratching their head!

Ronaldo mainly uses the chop when he's got a defender beside or just behind him, and they're both running in a forward direction. When he changes direction, it takes a beat for the defender to work out what's happened – and by then, Ronaldo's long gone!

THE RONALDO CHOP

(REAL MADRID V AS ROMA, UEFA CHAMPIONS LEAGUE, 2016

WE'RE 57 MINUTES INTO THIS LAST 16 GAME AND IT'S STILL 0–0. WHO WILL HIT THE BACK OF THE NET FIRST . . . ?

MARCELO TAKES THE BALL FOR REAL MADRID AND FINDS CRISTIANO RONALDO DOWN THE LEFT.

CR7'S OFF. HE'S MOTORING!

ROMA'S ALESSANDRO FLORENZI IS CLOSING IN . . .

CHOP!!

This jaw-dropping goal was voted the best of the 2015/2016 tournament!

KNEE CATCH

This skill might seem simple, but it'll show you've got amazing control of the ball! Don't worry if it takes you a while to get it – practice is all part of becoming an amazing freestyler.

1 Bounce the ball in front of you. Keep it low – you only want it to bounce up to around knee height.

2 As the ball bounces up, bend your knees a bit and pinch them together to catch it.

It might take a few goes to get the timing right, but keep trying – you'll get there!

3

Release the ball from between your knees. You could just let it fall and bounce, or add some flair with a little jump as you release.

Go straight into a juggle if you're feeling flashy!

Bounce

FREESTYLER FUN STUFF

Can you guess how many knee catches I did in 30 seconds to break the world record?

8   15   31

Answer on p125!

EXTRA-TIME CHALLENGE

Try putting this together with a Pullback Flick. See if you can flick the ball up and then do your Knee Catch!

HOTSTEPPER

Ready to test your hot-stepping stamina?
This high-energy skill's going to get
your heart pumping!

1

Start by practising a few high knees to get your body used to the movement.

Hop from foot to foot, lifting your knee as high as you can on each leg.

2 Grab your ball, then drop it and let it bounce up again. Keep things nice and gentle, so the ball doesn't bounce too high.

3

As the ball's coming up from its bounce, lift your knee high and tap the top of the ball with the sole of your foot, so it goes into another bounce.

Tap 👣

4

If you're feeling pumped, try hopping straight to the other leg and catching the new bounce with a tap of your other foot. How many taps can you manage before you lose control of the ball?

Focus on control if you want to be an extra-spicy Hotstepper. If you stamp hard on that ball, it's going to bounce back too high for you to get your next foot on top of it!

ROOKIE

SCISSOR FLICK-UP

Whichever way you *cut* it (GROAN) a Scissor Flick-up is a snappy way to get the ball in the air. You've got to be *sharp* with your feet for this one! (DOUBLE GROAN!)

1

Jump up with both feet, and land with one foot either side of the ball.

2

Do another jump (a tiny one this time) and snap both feet together as quickly as you can. The speed will help you get your feet underneath the ball.

Smile 😀

REF'S RIDDLE

Which football megastar is known for his fancy flick-ups on the pitch? Grab a pen and paper to solve the ref's riddle!

Here's a clue – he's from Brazil!

The first letter of my name is in **pen** but not in **pet**.

The second letter is in **step** but not in **stop**.

The third is in **sky** but not in **ski**.

The fourth letter is in **megged** but not in **begged**.

The fifth is in **ball** but not in **bull**.

The sixth is in **prop** but not in **plop**.

Answer on p125!

NUTMEG

No one wants to hear 'MEGGGGS!' during a kick-about – it means you've been tricked!

A **nutmeg** (also known as a **panna**) is when a playe tricks their opponent by sending a ball through their legs, then runs round them to collect the ball and carry on running.

NUTMEG KNOW-HOW

You

Opponent

Big gap!

While you're dribbling, keep your head up and eyes peeled for that crucial gap between a defender's legs.

Remember – no one can run with their legs together!

Nutmeg 👍

If your touch is **too soft**, the defender will get to the ball before it goes through their legs. If it's **too hard**, it'll end up reaching another defender on the other side!

The right touch will come with practice.

PANNA PRANK

Even if you're not ready to meg yet, you can still prank a mate. You'll need two balls, and you'll have to wait till they're not looking!

1. Pass a ball so they have to stretch out for it.

2. As they stretch for the first ball, quickly pass the second ball straight through their open legs!

3. Call 'MEGS!' and enjoy the confused look on their face!

TRUE OR FALSE?

There's a Panna World Championships, where doing a meg means an instant win!

Answer on p125!

Check out me pranking a robot friend of mine by scanning the QR code.

THE ALESSIA RUSSO NUTMEG
(ENGLAND V SWEDEN, UEFA WOMEN'S EUROS, 2022)

THERE'S TWENTY-TWO MINUTES LEFT TO PLAY IN THIS THRILLING SEMI-FINAL! ENGLAND ARE 2–0 UP AND THE FINAL IS IN REACH FOR THE LIONESSES, BUT SWEDEN COULD STILL PULL IT BACK . . .

IT'S FRAN KIRBY IN THE PENALTY AREA. LOVELY CROSS TO ALESSIA RUSSO.

RUSSO TAKES THE SHOT . . . AN IMPRESSIVE SAVE FROM SWEDISH KEEPER HEDVIG LINDAHL.

RUSSO WINS THE BALL, AND — WHOAAAA!

A BACKHEEL! *HAS ANYONE TOLD ALESSIA RUSSO THIS IS A EUROS SEMI-FINAL?! SHE'S ICE COLD!*

AND A DOUBLE MEGS! RUUUUSSSOOOOOO!

MARCELO TOUCH

Famous Brazilian left-back Marcelo had an ice-cold first touch. Practise this skill for long enough and you might become famous for your ball control too.

1

As your teammate sends you a lofted pass, lift your foot a little.

Lofted pass

Just before the ball lands, bring your foot down to stop it dead, sandwiching it between the sole of your foot and the ground. Timing has to be SPOT ON here, and you might not get it right first time. Keep trying!

2

3

Flick the ball out and run off with it. Or, roll it under the sole of your foot as you turn to face the direction you want to go in. Then run off. Either way, you'll look like a total boss!

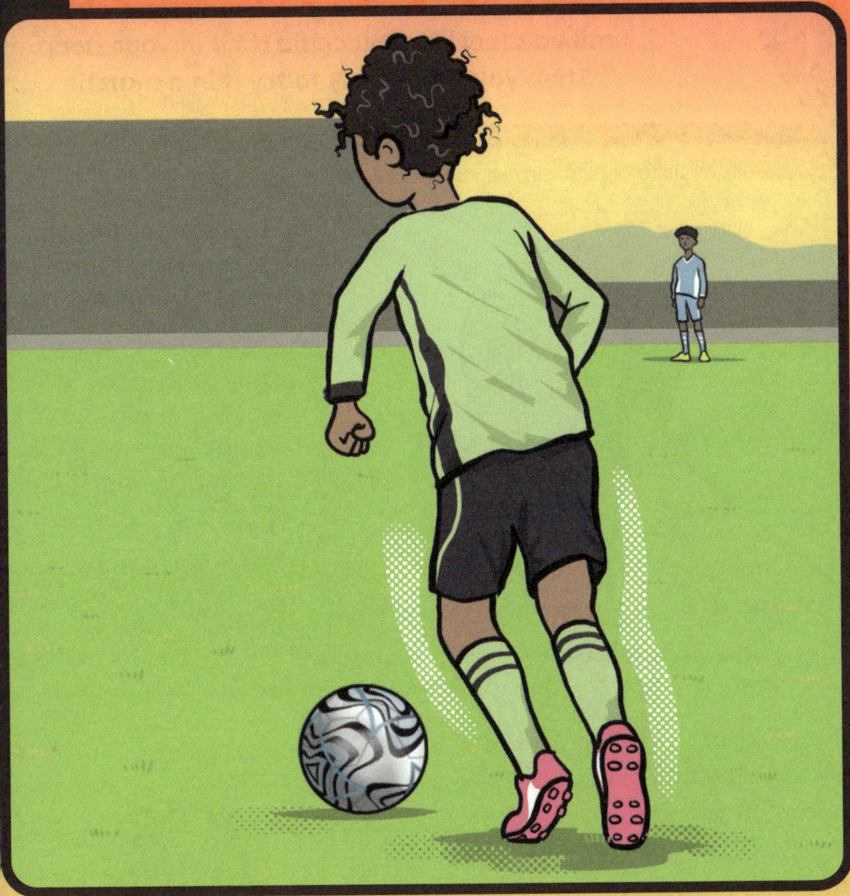

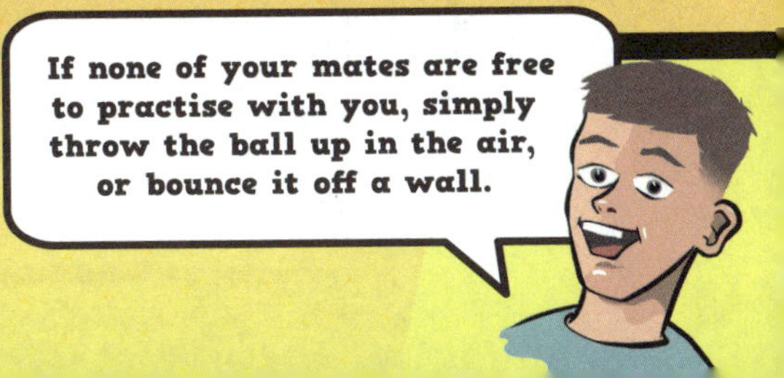

If none of your mates are free to practise with you, simply throw the ball up in the air, or bounce it off a wall.

STEPOVERS

This is one of my top defender-dodging skills!
The Stepover is one to practise and practise,
until you feel like you could do it in your sleep.
Then you'll be ready to try it in a match!

1 Start by getting used to the movement. It's like you're drawing an upside-down smile with your foot, just a little bit off the ground. Do it with one foot, then the other. When you've done it lots of times, see if you can speed up

2

Now put the ball in front of you and practise the same movement around it. Make sure you don't touch the ball with either foot!

3 Let's take it to the next level. Dribble for a few touches. Then plant the inside of your weak foot beside the ball and do the stepover movement with your strong foot.

Quickly tap the ball away with your weak foot and follow its new direction!

Strong leg

Tap 🦶

EXTRA-TIME CHALLENGE

Reckon you could beat a world-record-breaker? Back in 2014, Ash Randall showed his stepover tekkers by doing a whopping **127** in one minute! (The kind where the ball stays still, like in Step 2.)

How many can you do?

NECK STALL

Show off your ice-cool control with this freestyle skill. How long can you balance for? Find a mate and time each other!

1

With the ball at your feet, stand with your legs apart and your knees soft. Hinge at your hips and fold forward with a flat back. Look out ahead of you, not down to the ground.

2

Lift your elbows to make chicken wings with your arms. It'll create a groove for the ball between your shoulder blades.

Pick up the ball and put it against the back of your head. When it's balanced, quickly make those wings to hold it in the groove!

EXTRA-TIME CHALLENGE

Once you're a ball-balancing boss, why not try a **Neck Flick-Up**?

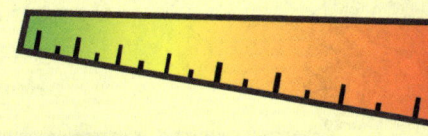

1

Bend your knees a little and look down at the ground. The ball will start rolling along the back of your head.

2 Quickly straighten your legs and lift your body at the same time as you flick your head up. The movement will send the ball into the air above you, so you can catch it!

Flick ☝️

ELASTICO

Up next is a dribbling trick you might
have already tried on *EA FC*!
Here's how to do it for real.

1

Push the ball
out with the
outside of
your foot.

2

As you push, drop
your shoulder and
lean out a bit to trick
the defender into
thinking you're going
in the same direction
as the ball.

3

Quickly plant the same foot on the other side of the ball, with your toes angled slightly inwards. Push the ball back the other way, this time using the inside of your foot.

4

Take the ball with your other foot and continue dribbling down the pitch, leaving the defence for dust!

EXTRA-TIME CHALLENGE

THE REVERSE ELASTICO

Keep those defenders guessing by throwing in a reverse version. In Step 1, instead of pushing the ball out first, push it in then out. Follow the ball with your shoulder, like the OG version.

Some people call this trick the Flip Flap!

IMPROVER

HOCUS POCUS

Want to make some footy freestyle magic?
Show off your Hocus Pocus tekkers and
you'll cast a spell over everyone!

1 Plant your weak foot to the outside of the ball, a few centimetres in front of it.

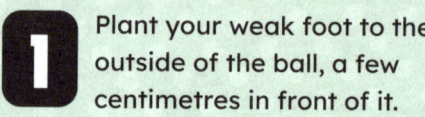

2 Gently tap the ball behind your planted foot with the inside of your strong foot.

3 As the ball moves behind your planted weak foot, follow it with your strong foot. Then make a second touch using the laces of your strong foot.

4 Chase after that ball!

This is an attacking skill best done when you're moving slowly. Why not try it from a gentle dribble?

PILEDRIVER

This one's a great linking skill to learn for freestyle combos. It takes practice to find the right angle for your knee and how much force to use in the slam. But let's dig into it – you've got this!

1 Start by juggling. Or, just bounce the ball in front of you. (Turn to p12 if you want to learn to juggle first!)

2 As the ball rises to around knee height, bend your knee and make contact with the top of the ball.

3

Slam the ball back down to the ground using the top of your shin/knee. Give it some welly!

4

Plant your foot back on the ground and let the ball bounce once. Catch it with a foot or hands. If you're feeling confident, try it on one leg and then the other!

EXTRA-TIME CHALLENGE

Start with a Foot Stall (p22), tap the ball up and go straight into a Piledriver. It might take a few tries to get the height of the ball right for the Piledriver slam, but don't worry – practice really helps with this combo.

To stop the ball BOINGing off in the wrong direction, make sure your shin is as close to parallel to the ground as you can make it when you slam the ball down.

POPCORN FLICK

Like my favourite movie snack, this skill's POPPIN'! It's a great way to pop the ball off the ground and up into the air with style.

1

Plant your weak foot a step ahead of the ball. Keep both knees soft.

2

Put the toe of your strong foot on top of the ball.

3 Roll the ball back using your toes. You'll end up with your laces touching the back side of the ball.

4 Quickly scoop your toes under the ball. At the same time, pop your leg straight out behind you. Watch that ball flick up and forward!

FREESTYLER FUN STUFF

Star Swedish player Zlatan Ibrahimović made the popcorn flick famous. He holds the record for the most goals scored for Sweden in the men's game*. Can you guess how many?

12

39

62

*Including a RIDICULOUS bicycle kick against England, 30 yards from goal! Look it up – you can thank me later ☺

Answer on p125!

IMPROVER

RAINBOW FLICK

Sometimes, the only way out of a tight spot is with an arching overhead flick. Learn to make a rainbow with the ball and you might find a pot of gold at the end of it! (Or maybe a pot of GOAL! ☺)

1 Squeeze the ball between your ankles, just like you did in Step 1 of the Rocket Launcher (p20).

2 Use the inside of your strong foot to roll the ball up the inside of your opposite calf. It can help the motion to press into the ball with your foot a bit.

IMPROVER

3 As you're rolling the ball up, jump off your weak foot and quickly lift your weak heel towards your bum.

4 Land your strong foot back down as the ball arcs up into the air – maybe even over your shoulder!

EXTRA-TIME CHALLENGE

Once you're comfy with the motion and timing of the roll and flick, try to put as much power as you can on the flick part. Make sure you're leaning forward a bit too, so the ball is sent in an arch shape overhead, not just straight up in the air.

THE MARTA FLICK-UP
(BRAZIL V USA, FIFA WORLD CUP, 2007)

REWIND TO 2007 AND WOMEN'S FOOTBALL'S
GREATEST RIVALS MEETING IN THE WORLD CUP
SEMI-FINAL. MARTA, THE BRAZILIAN WITH THE BEST
TEKKERS IN THE WORLD, HAS ALREADY SCORED ONE,
BUT THE USA DEFENCE IS AT HER BACK . . .

CRISTIANE LOFTS IT TO HER STRIKE PARTNER, MARTA. HOW'S
MARTA GOING TO FIND SPACE TO DO ANYTHING WITH IT?

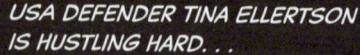

USA DEFENDER TINA ELLERTSON
IS HUSTLING HARD. . .

OH!

PURE INSTINCT AND PURE GENIUS! MARTA DOESN'T BLINK – IT'S STRAIGHT INTO A BEAUTIFUL ARCHING FLICK-UP!

SHE'S FOXED ELLERTSON, AND NOW SHE'S FOXED DEFENDER WHITEHILL.

COULD THIS BE A SECOND GOAL FOR BRAZIL'S SUPERSTAR . . . ?

YES IT CANNNNNNN! TEAM USA HAD NO HOPE AGAINST THIS ONCE-IN-A-LIFETIME TALENT!

CRUYFF TURN

Dutch player Johan Cruyff invented this direction-changing move to ditch a defender in the 1974 World Cup. Try it in a game and you'll shake off your opponent in no time!

1

Draw your strong foot back like you're about to shoot or pass the ball. Make sure your weak foot is planted in front of the ball.

2

Instead of following through to boot the ball, stop your strong foot sharply beside it. Cut the ball behind your weak leg with the inside of your strong foot. It helps to angle your toes in a bit.

3 Quickly turn your body 180 degrees in the direction of the defender and carry on with the ball. The defender will probably take a couple of steps the wrong way while you head on to goal!

FREESTYLER FUN STUFF

Johan Cruyff has a skill with his name on, but what else has been named after him?

You've got to be a good actor for this skill to work. The defender needs to think you're going to take a shot or make a pass BEFORE you turn, so give Step 1 all the drama you can!

Answer on p125!

| A baby panda | An asteroid | An energy drink |

McGEADY SPIN

Cool with Cruyff? Then let's move with McGeady! It's a great skill to have in your kitbag for when a defender's at your back. They'll follow the first touch, but you've got a sneaky second coming right up to fool them!

Smash Step 1 and 2 of a Cruyff Turn (p58). Don't forget to show off your acting skills!

1

2

This time, as you make the 180-degree turn towards the defender, use the outside of your weak foot to tap the ball away to the side

3 Speed is crucial – if you can put these two touches together super fast, you'll leave your opponent for dust! Top tekkers!

Irish player Aiden McGeady took the Cruyff Turn and levelled it up. The McGeady Spin has even made it into *EA FC*, where it's a 5-star skill move.

IMPROVER

BAMBINI*

This one's just for laughs. Don't try it in a match or you might get in trouble with the ref!

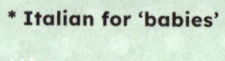
* Italian for 'babies'

1 Start by juggling with your strong foot.

2 Kick the ball high, to around level with your chest.

3 Grab the bottom of your shirt or top and pull it out to catch the ball.

62

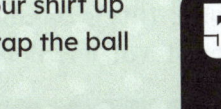

4 Immediately toss the ball back in the air with your shirt, and as it comes down, pull your shirt up then out to trap the ball underneath.

5 Showboat for your mates as they crease up laughing!

FREESTYLER FUN STUFF

Doing the Bambini then running with the ball still up your shirt is banned by FIFA! Players can get a yellow card just for celebrating with a ball up their shirt. **Can you guess which of these ISN'T banned by FIFA?**

Answer on p125!

Make sure you're wearing a loose-fitting top for this trick. You don't want to stretch your fresh new team shirt with your ball 'baby'!

Goalie trying to distract a player taking a penalty.

Accidental hand balls.

Running with the ball in a Knee Catch.

RABONA

Who wants to just *kick* a ball, when you can do a Rabona! This is an uber-cool way to pass or shoot. You'll look like a total pro!

1 Plant your weak foot with the ball to the outside, about 30 cm away. Make sure your knees are soft and your toes are pointing in the direction you want the ball to go next.

2 Swing your strong leg round the back of your weak leg. Lean away from the ball a bit for better balance and an easier swing.

3 Strike the ball with your toes, or the laces area of your boot for power. Or, if you want to chip the ball, scoop your toes underneath a bit to get some height on it.

If it feels like there's not enough room for a proper leg swing in Step 2, make sure your foot is planted far enough away from the ball in Step 1.

HYPER PASS

Believe the hype – get this pass right and you'll feel all kinds of chuffed with yourself!

1
Plant your weak foot and place the sole of your strong foot on the ball.

2
Roll the ball back until it's out of line with your weak leg.

3

Scoop the ball up with the inside of your strong foot.

4 Send the ball off to the side as a pass.

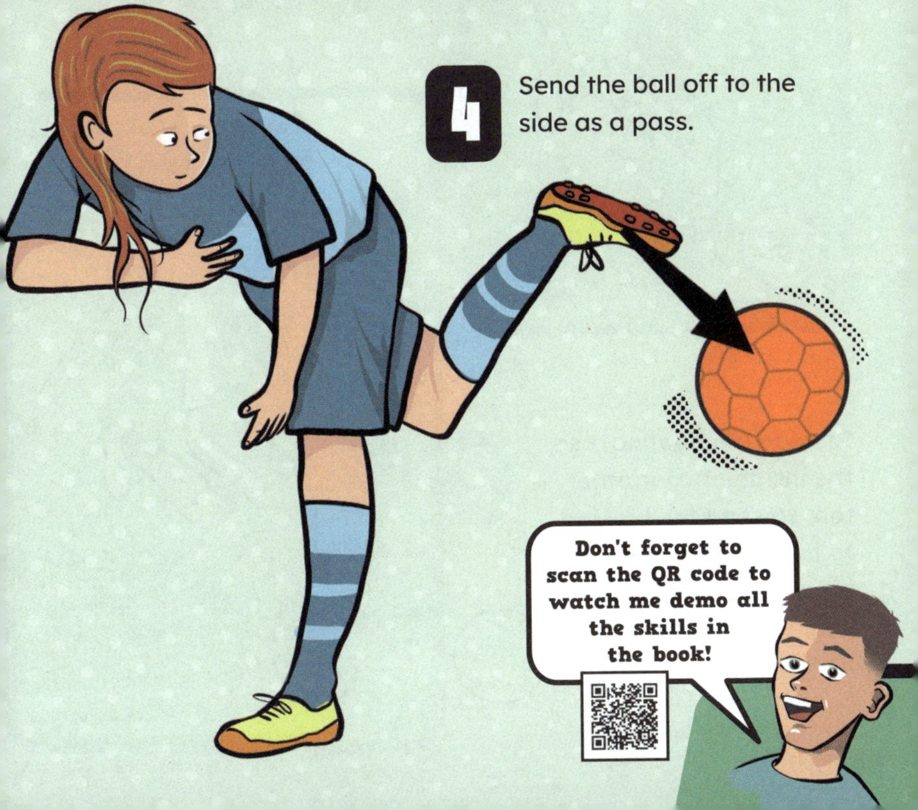

Don't forget to scan the QR code to watch me demo all the skills in the book!

HENRY FAKE PASS

In 2006, fans went crazy when French player Thierry Henry did his fake pass for the first time. It'd never been seen before! Who will you bamboozle with yours?

1 Take a run up to the ball like you're about to take a shot. Like with the Cruyff Turn (p54), you'll need your best acting skills to convince your opponent!

Instead of shooting, use the inside of your other foot to send the ball out to the side. Make this bit as low-key as you can, to keep the fake going.

2

3 As the ball leaves your foot, immediately swing your other leg through as if you're still taking a shot (even though the ball's not there now). The defence won't know which way to go!

4 Watch your teammate take advantage of the gap in the defence, pick up the pass and *scorrrrre!*

To make sure the defender stays clueless, don't look in the direction you're sending the ball in Step 2. With practice, you'll be able to predict the space a teammate can run into to collect the ball, before you even take the trick shot!

Answer on p125!

REF'S RIDDLE Like many top strikers, Henry was also a super-speedy runner. Sprinting in a game in 1998, he briefly hit a top speed that would have worried Usain Bolt! What speed did he reach?

| 39.2 km/h | 10 km/h | 21 km/h |

THE THIERRY HENRY FAKE PASS
(ARSENAL V MIDDLESBOROUGH, 2006)

WE'RE WELL INTO THE PREMIER LEAGUE 2005/2006 SEASON, AND ARSENAL ARE HAMMERING MIDDLESBOROUGH 6–0. THIERRY HENRY HAS ALREADY SCORED A HAT-TRICK. WHAT ELSE DOES HE HAVE UP HIS SLEEVE?

IT'S ASHLEY COLE TO HENRY ON THE RIGHT.

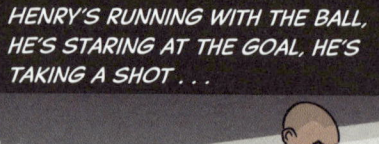

HENRY'S RUNNING WITH THE BALL, HE'S STARING AT THE GOAL, HE'S TAKING A SHOT . . .

Thierry Henry pulled this off so well the first time, he even tricked the camera person! The camera went one way, but the ball went the other!

HAMSTRING CATCH

In freestyle, this move is a type of 'blocking' skill. That's where a ball is caught and held by a part of the lower body. Here, the blocking body parts are the hamstring and the calf!

1

Start by getting used to the position. Bend your leg up and place the ball between the calf and hamstring, like this.

Hamstring

Calf

2 Bounce the ball or flick it up to waist height. Lift your heel towards your bum to catch the ball and trap it tightly between your calf and hamstring.

It can help to turn your upper body slightly to look back at your leg.

3 Release the ball and try it on the other leg. You could go into it from a juggle once you're feeling confident!

Timing is important in the Hamstring Catch, but so is the height of your heel. Lift it too high and the ball will bounce off your leg as there's no room for it to fit. Too low and it will slip through the gap between your heel and your hamstring.

EXTRA-TIME CHALLENGE

Putting blocking moves together is called a 'blocking combo'. See if you can try this blocking combo for beginners.

1) Do a knee catch (p28).

2) Release the ball and let it drop, but catch it between your ankles before it hits the ground. *Nice!*

POP PASS

Now you're a blocking boss with the Hamstring Catch, let's use those hammies again for this showboaty trick!

1

Toss the ball up to about shoulder height. Turn your body away from it and bring one knee towards your chest. Look over your shoulder to keep an eye on where the ball is.

2

When the ball drops to around hip height, tip your torso forward and kick your leg straight out behind you. Flex your foot and make the kick sharp, like you're trying to put your heel through a wall.*

***Check you've got space behind you first, and definitely *don't* kick a wall!**

IMPROVER

3

If your timing and leg position is good, the ball will pop right off your hamstring and into the air! Getting both things spot on takes lots of practice, but it's SO satisfying when you get it right!

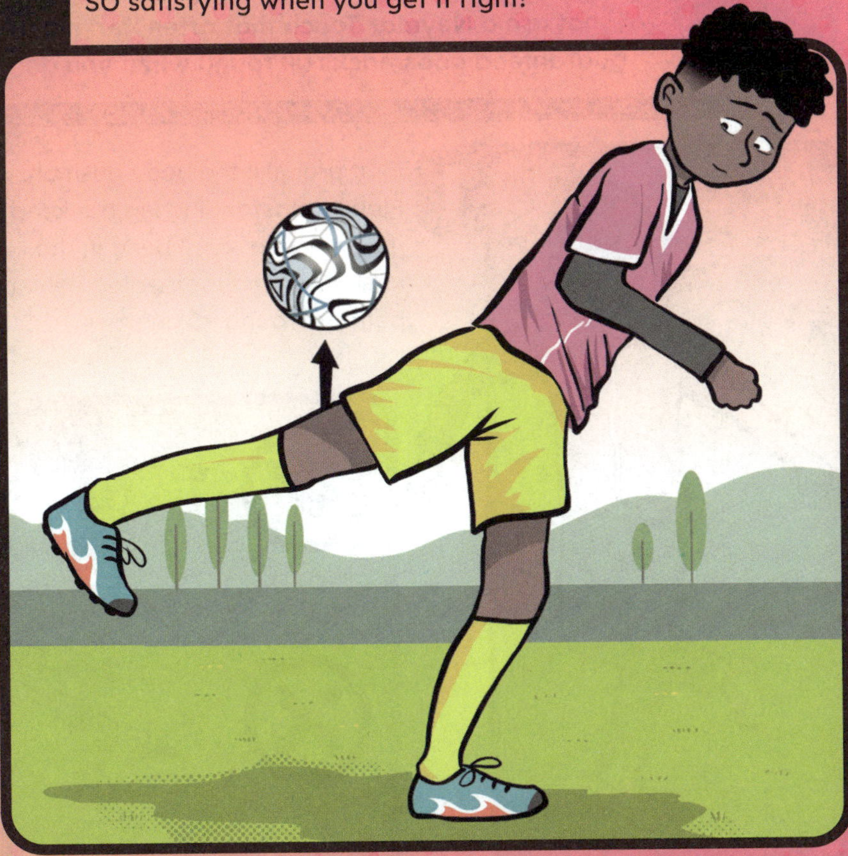

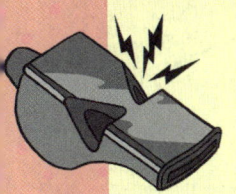

EXTRA-TIME CHALLENGE

Feeling extra flashy? Try a quick spin in a circle after the ball's popped off your hamstring, then catch it with your foot and go into a juggle!

NEYMAR TOUCH

Commentators are left speechless by Neymar's control when he receives the ball! You might not use a Neymar Touch that often, but it's guaranteed gobsmacks all round when you do.

1 First practise the body position. Plant your standing leg but keep it soft, with a small bend in the knee. Bring your other leg behind, bent at around 90 degrees.

2 Now make sure your foot is at the best angle. You're aiming for about 45 degrees, to stop the ball pinging off in a direction you don't want!

3 Toss the ball up in the air and practise receiving it with the inside of your lifted foot. Remember 'cushioning' from the Foot Stall (p23)? Move your foot back gently as the ball lands, to cushion it and kill the ball. Otherwise, it'll BOING off without any control.

4 When you're confident, get a mate to send you a cross. Do Steps 1–3 for a ball-killing Neymar Touch!

FREESTYLER FUN STUFF

Megastar Lionel Messi also has a superhuman first touch. On Japanese TV, he shocked the world when he lofted a ball over a high barrier, ran underneath and then controlled the ball on the other side with his first touch.

How high was the barrier?

3.05 metres
(the height of a pro basketball hoop)

5.49 metres
(3 of me, standing on my own shoulders!)

18 metres
(just over 4 double decker buses stacked on top of each other!)

Answer on p125!

PRO

PRO

HOP AKKA

You'll spot this skill in the fast and furious game of panna, where the play is one-on-one. Panna pros have to bust out some intense tricks to get around their opponent! Let's break it down.

1 Trap the ball between your ankles (like in Rocket Launcher on p20). Practise jumping side to side with it trapped.

2 Now do Step 1 but release the ball with your strong leg. Make sure you're jumping to the same side as your strong leg. You can lean your body to the opposite side, to make sure you're getting enough height before the release.

3 Then add the kick. As you release, extend your strong leg to kick the ball out in front of you. You're sort of hooking it with your foot as you kick, so aim for the laces area.

4 Add in an opponent! Kick the ball past them on one side, and run round them on the other to collect the ball and carry on. See you later, defence!

You 👇

Ball ⚽

EXTRA-TIME CHALLENGE

Try this with a few steps of run up. For the trap part, do a little jump into it, landing your feet either side of the ball and squeezing tight. That'll help you keep the momentum going.

If you don't have a mate to practise with, just use something that doesn't move as your opponent, like a chair!

AROUND THE WORLD

Let's go global with this super impressive trick. Make sure you've got your juggling skills nice and sharp first (check out p12) – a real pro does their Around the Worlds from a controlled juggle!

1 Begin by juggling, or, to start off easy, just balance the ball on the top of your foot.

2 Lift your knee up to 90 degrees. Let the ball roll to the outside of your foot – just for a split second.

3 Now whip your leg around the ball in a circle. Make it lightning fast! Aim for your lower leg to be going around the ball, not your thigh.

4 Catch the ball on top of your foot before it hits the ground, and pop it back up into a juggle. You've got to be snappy with your circle to get your foot back in place for the catch!

EXTRA-TIME CHALLENGE

Once you get really good, you can string Around the Worlds together in a row! Scan the QR code to watch me show you how.

Struggling to nail this one? Take it right back to basics . . . First, make sure your standing leg is really solid, then practise speedy leg circles without the ball. Then skip Steps 1 and 2 and drop the ball in front of you instead, to get the feel for the speed you'll need in your circle.

AIR JESTER

If fancy footwork is your style, you're going to love this freestyle trick! It's using part of the Around the World skill that you just learnt, so you're already halfway there.

1 Start juggling. Catch the ball with your strong foot, lift your knee and very briefly let the ball roll to the *inside* of that foot.

2 Start an Around the World circle with your strong foot. This time, you're making the circle *inwards* around the ball. Think of it as leading with your inner thigh. FYI – you're only going to go halfway with your circle in this trick.

At the same time as you start your circle, jump off the weak foot and cross it beneath your strong leg.

4

Bring your weak foot up to meet the ball and tap it back into the air.

Land on your weak leg and catch the ball underneath with your strong foot. Finish where you started – juggling!

5

FREESTYLER FUN STUFF

Step 3 is a skill on its own, known as a Crossover. Turn to p118 for the story of how I broke a world crossovers record!

SOMBRERO FLICK

This one's named after a hat with a really wide brim that is worn in Mexico. The kick part of the trick has to be in a nice big arc so you don't hit your sombrero on the way over!

1 Place the toes of your strong foot under the ball as much as you can without making it roll away. Your weak foot should be behind you.

Spring off your weak foot. You're aiming to land the foot in front of the ball, but not until Step 4. ☺

2

Scan the code to watch me demo the trick!

3 Before your weak foot lands, lift your strong foot up with your knee bent. Imagine a string attached to the top of your knee, pulling it directly upwards. The ball will flick up with it.

4

Land on your weak foot and quickly extend your strong leg to make contact with the ball. Aim for the laces part of your foot. Lean your body back a bit as you extend the leg.

5 Kick the ball back over your head. Keep your eyes on it as it sails over you.

6 Quickly turn in the opposite direction and try to catch the ball!

EXTRA-TIME CHALLENGE

Can you try it with a run-up? With practice, you'll get used to where you need to place your strong foot so the ball won't roll away.

NECK STALL PRESS-UP

You've already bossed the Neck Stall way back in the Rookie section. Now you're a Pro, it's time to add more spice to those chicken wings!

1 Get into the Neck Stall position from p42. Balance a ball in the groove created by your chicken-wing arms.

2 Keeping your eyes forward and your upper body super still, carefully lower yourself to a bent-over kneeling position. Take it one knee at a time. Don't look down at the ground, or that'll make your head dip!

3

Lower your hands to the ground, keeping the rest of your body as still as you can to stop the ball rolling off your back. Keep looking forward.

Carefully stretch one leg out behind you, then the other, lifting into a plank position. Unlike in a plank,

4 you need to stick your bum in the air a bit to help the ball stay on your back!

Lower into a press-up. If you aren't ready for full press-ups, don't plank in Step 4 – just raise

5 your heels after you've stretched out your legs and press up from your knees.

EXTRA-TIME CHALLENGE

For the ultimate control challenge, try this short and steady combo:

1) Neck Stall Press-Up

2) Reverse the steps, back up to a Neck Stall position

3) Neck Flick-Up (from p43)

For pro press-up form, hands should be beneath your shoulders with your fingers pointing forward. As you do the press-up, think about tightening your core and glute muscles and keep your elbows pointing outwards as much as you can.

RAINBOW 360

This is the Rainbow Flick from p54, but with a twist – literally! You want a bit of momentum for this trick as you're going to be turning through 360 degrees, so try going into Step 1 while dribbling.

As you reach the ball, start turning your body at the same time as you go to trap it between your feet.

You'll turn **anti-clockwise** if your strong leg is your RIGHT one, and **clockwise** if it's your LEFT.

1

Anti-clockwise

2 Keep the turn going as you roll the ball up your calf with your strong foot. Don't forget to press the foot into the ball a bit to help with the roll.

3 Keep turning as you jump off your weak foot and lift the weak heel towards your bum to make contact with the ball and flick it up in the air.

4 A full turn should be nearly complete by the time you land your strong foot down.

5 Chase down the ball!

Finding it tricky to trap the ball from a running start AND turn at the same time?! Think about bringing your strong foot round the outside of the ball as you start to turn your body. Then use your strong foot to guide the ball *to* your weak foot, putting pressure on to trap it there.

MARADONA 7

FIFA's joint Player of the 20th Century, Diego Maradona, could control the ball with pretty much any part of his body! This trick named after him uses seven body parts. Can you match Maradona with your control tekkers?

1 Do a kick-up with one foot, then the other. Send the second kick-up to around knee height.

2 Do a keepy-uppy with your thigh. Repeat with the other thigh. Send the second keepy-uppy to shoulder height. Keep your eyes fixed on the ball!

3 Get under the ball with one shoulder. Pop your shoulder up just as the ball touches it, to send the ball into the air. Keep your arm tucked into your side. You don't want to fling it out as you pop!

4 Repeat with the other shoulder. The movement should be like a one-shoulder shrug!

5 Finish with the cherry on top – a header!

6 If this is too tricky to start with, catch the ball with your hands between each set of body parts. So: one foot, other foot, catch. One thigh, other thigh, catch. One shoulder, other shoulder, catch. Header, catch.

REF'S RIDDLE

What did Maradona's handball goal become known as?

The Hand of Diego

The Hand of God

The Hand of What's VAR*?

*Video Assistant Referee (it hadn't been invented in 1986!)

In 1986, Maradona helped to knock England out of the World Cup with two iconic goals. The body part he used for goal one was his left hand, and even though a handball's totally illegal, the ref and the linesman still gave it! WHAAAT?!

Answer on p125!

PRO

AIR ELASTICO

Remember the Elastico from p44? This is the same in-and-out movement, just with added air!

1 Start with a juggle or a regular flick-up.

2 When the ball's at the height of your mid shin, push it out to the side with the outer bit of your foot.

Make it quick ⚡

3 Sharply extend your leg to catch the ball with the inside of your foot before it hits the ground, sending the ball back across your body.

EXTRA-TIME CHALLENGE

Want to make your Air Elastico *SUPER* Pro?
Swap Step 1 for this flick-up – it comes direct from
the boot of the Brazilian Elastico boss, Ronaldinho.

1 Plant your weak foot, then use your strong foot to roll the ball onto your weak foot. Your strong leg will end up crossed over your weak leg.

2

As soon as the ball touches your weak foot, lift the toes to flick it up. The whole movement should be super quick.

Lift ⬆ ⬆ ⬆

SITTING JUGGLE

Take a load off your feet with this impressive freestyle trick. It took practice, but eventually I could show off my Sitting Juggle for ages without dropping the ball!

1

Sit on the floor with your knees pointing to the sky and your feet flat on the ground.

2

Drop the ball over one foot and gently tap it back up to catch. Keep your ankle locked and your tapping foot straight. Aim to tap with the laces area.

3 Repeat on the other foot. Then try two taps in a row on one foot with a catch, then two on the other with a catch. And then try tapping it from one foot to the other before catching.

4 When you're feeling confident, it's time to let your feet handle the hard work. Plant your hands either side of you for support and juggle for as long as you can! How many taps can you do in a row? Keep trying to beat your record!

FREESTYLER FUN STUFF

Agim Agushi broke the world record for a different sitting juggle – the longest while using his head! He managed a mega 4 hours, 2 minutes and 1 second! **Which of these is another record smashed by Agim?**

1) The most headers scored while blindfolded.

2) The most times taking off and putting on a T-shirt while controlling the ball with his head.

3) The most sitting juggles with a golf ball.

To save having to get up to collect the ball every time, practise facing a wall. The ball will just roll back to you when your control goes wonky!

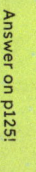

Answer on p125!

SOLE STALL

Now we're going from sitting to lying down. (Who knew football could be so chill?!) The Sole Stall will test your control skills to the limit, but when you've mastered it, no one will believe you haven't just glued the ball to your shoe!

1 Lie on your back with your knees pointing upwards and palms flat on the ground either side. Engage your core muscles and lift your head.

2 Now practise getting into the full Sole Stall position. Lift your strong leg so your body makes a L shape.

Keep your strong foot flat and a sof bend in your strong knee.

3 Time to add in the ball! In the Step 1 position, throw it into the air. As you throw, lift your leg into the Step 2 position and try to catch the ball on the front part of your sole. How long can you keep it up there?

4 Make tiny adjustments with your leg and your foot to try and keep the ball balanced. With practice, you'll know exactly how to move to stop the ball rolling off.

You could even practise this one while lying in bed!

5 Repeat Step 3 and 4 over and over and over and . . . 😁

PRO

SLAP

Like the name says – this freestyle trick slaps! ☺
It's not one you'll use in a match, but it's
amazing in a freestyle combo. I like to
break it out when I need a linking move.

1 Squeeze the ball between your ankles.

2 Using your strong foot to guide it, roll
the ball around the back of your weak
ankle, to the outside. Apply pressure
with the laces area of your strong foot
the whole time to hold the ball there.

3

Sharply roll the ball up your weak calf with your strong foot, then release it.

Release! ⭐

4

Turn your body towards the ball with your strong leg still lifted.

5

Catch the ball with your strong foot and juggle. You can also put your strong foot down after Step 4 and juggle with your weak foot instead!

Don't be tempted to jump off your standing leg in Step 3, otherwise the ball will ping off too far for you to catch and juggle!

BICYCLE KICK

You'll need a soft landing to practise this flashy trick. I learnt on a blow-up mattress in my mum's garden. ☺ You'll have your back to goal when you do it in a game, so the keeper will never predict a ball is coming their way! SCORRRRRRE!

1 Start by practising a high knee. Take a step forward and spring up off your strong foot. Lift your weak knee so your thigh's almost parallel to the ground.

2 Now try Step 1 without the spring up, but this time, lean your body back as you lift the weak knee.

PRO

3 Put Steps 1 and 2 together, but this time, as you spring off your strong foot, drive it through into a high kick.

Finally, add in the ball. You want to hit it with the top of your foot, where the laces are. Toss the ball in the air and practise timing your high kick so your laces hit the ball as it drops. You're a bicycle-kicking boss!

4

To protect your back and head once you get out onto the pitch, stick out your arms before you land. Your hands will hit the ground before your back and take some of the load.

THE SYDNEY LEROUX BICYCLE KIC
(ANGEL CITY FC V PORTLAND THORNS FC, 2023)

WE'RE IN LOS ANGELES FOR HOME TEAM ANGEL CITY'S GAME AGAINST PORTLAND. LA'S WOMEN ARE 3-0 UP AND ON THE ATTACK!

SCARLETT CAMBEROS PICKS UP A LONG BALL FOR ACFC AND SPRINTS INTO THE PENALTY AREA, SLOWING THINGS DOWN FOR JUST A SECOND. SHE TAKES A SHOT . . .

NO LUCK. IT BOUNCES OFF THE GLOVES OF KEEPER BELLA BIXBY.

WAIT. SYDNEY LEROUX HAS FOUND SOME SPACE. BUT SHE'S FACING AWAY FROM GOAL . . .

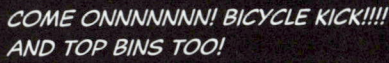

COME ONNNNNNN! BICYCLE KICK!!!!
AND TOP BINS TOO!

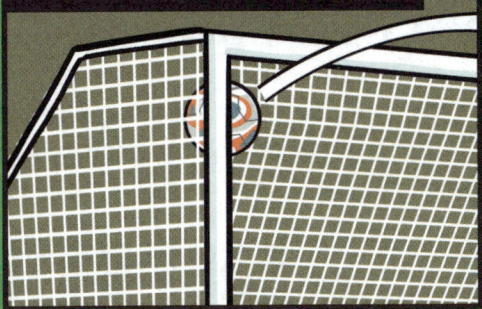

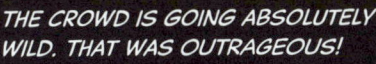

THE CROWD IS GOING ABSOLUTELY
WILD. THAT WAS OUTRAGEOUS!

**Leroux's goal helped her team go through to the
National Women's Soccer League Championship
playoffs for the very first time.**

FREESTYLE COMBOS

Now you've got all the tekkers, why not try putting some of them together! Here's a couple of quick freestyle combos to get you started.

EASY DOES IT . . .

p16

p22

JUGGLE

FOOT STALL

FLICK-UP

BAMBINI

p62

BIT MORE TRICKY!

p18

p28

p54

p20

PULLBACK FLICK

KNEE CATCH

ANKLE SQUEEZE
(ROCKET
LAUNCHER)

RAINBOW FLICK

Can you choose some tricks from the book and build your own combo?

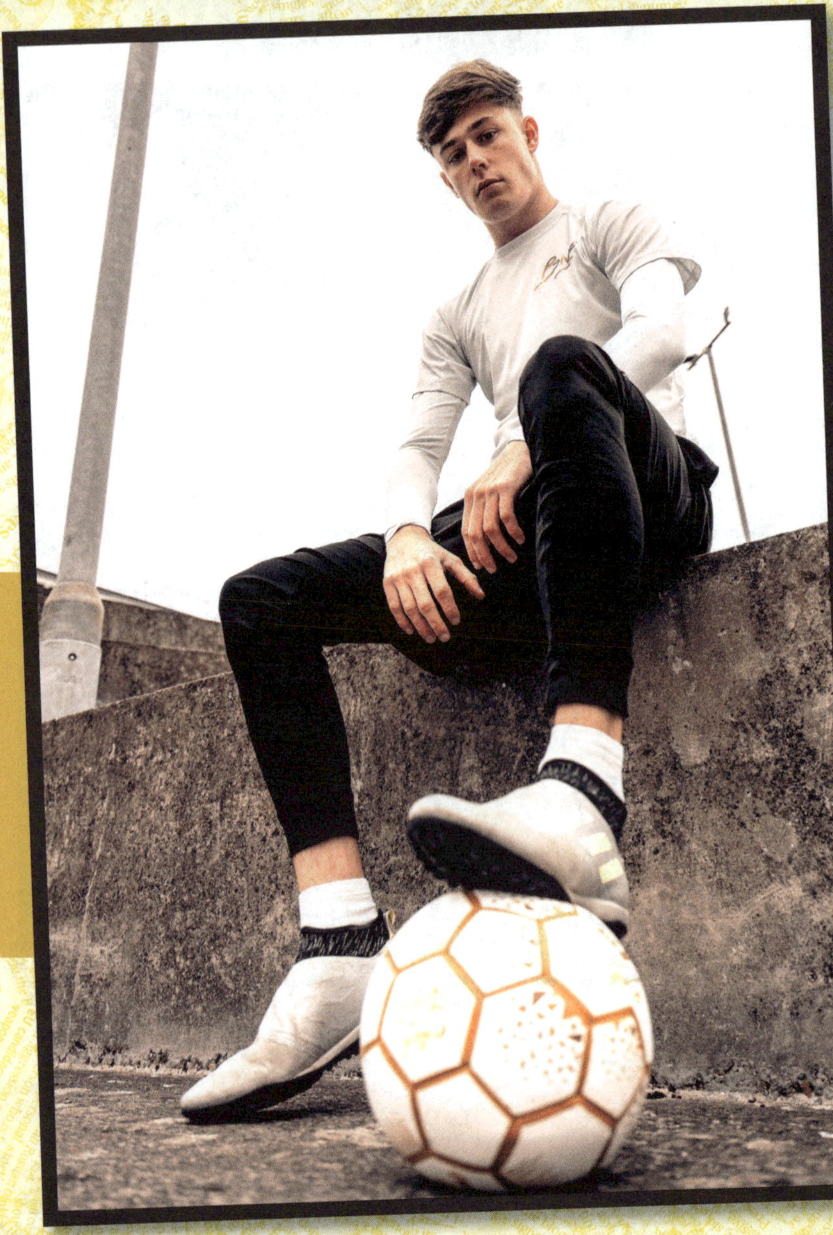

RECORD BREAKERS

When I was a kid, my mum used to buy me the Guinness World Records® book every year. I often thought how cool it would be to appear in the book myself, but it felt like an impossible dream! Then, when I started practising freestyle football and saw videos of people smashing Guinness World Records with awesome football skills, I realised it might be possible after all! After that, I would lie in bed every night thinking up records I could break.

MOST RUGBY BALL JUGGLES IN A ROW

Target to beat: 152

My very first world record attempt was held at Ormiston Academy, on 9th May, 2018. Lots of students and young footballers came to watch!

I was nervous, but I also had confidence in myself because I had practised every day for six months.

My goal for every practice session was to beat the target of 152 rugby ball foot touches in a row at least once.

I put in the hard work to give myself the best shot at making my dream come true!

It wasn't easy, but guess what happened?

I crushed that target, setting a new world record of **187**!

MOST FOOTBALL NECK-CATCH PASSES IN ONE MINUTE

Target to beat: 20

I was feeling so confident, I went for another record that same day! This time, it was with my mate Rebaz.

The two of us started freestyle at the same time, and were from the same area. We connected through social media and started practising for this record attempt together.

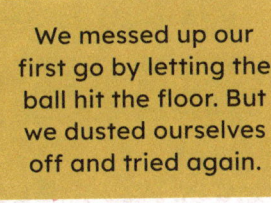

We messed up our first go by letting the ball hit the floor. But we dusted ourselves off and tried again.

On our second try we broke the record, with **41** passes between us in one minute!

Me and Rebaz went from strangers to friends, and then to joint Guinness World Record holders! ☺

MOST JUGGLES WHILE WEARING 5KG ANKLE WEIGHTS IN ONE MINUTE

Target to beat: 170

The team at Guinness World Records heard what I'd achieved and invited me to their HQ in London to make my third record attempt. Of course, I said yes!

This record was a tough one to practise. It took a lot of strength to keep my foot off the ground for a whole minute with a heavy weight strapped to it.

I knew I would only have three attempts on the day, and it was being livestreamed on the Guinness World Records social media channels. The pressure was on!

When I got to HQ, I ignored the cameras and locked in on the task in front of me. In the end, the minute sped by.

With **217** juggles, I smashed my third world record!

MOST FOOTBALL KNEE CATCHES IN 30 SECONDS

Target to beat: 23

Fast forward to the COVID lockdown. I had to find ways to keep busy, so what do you think I did? Yep, try to break more records! ☺ Because of the restrictions at the time, I had to film my fourth record attempt in my garden and send it in to Guinness World Records. They wanted it filmed from lots of different angles!

My brother, Luke, was in charge of timing and my mum was keeping count. It was really special that they could be there when I broke the record, with **31** knee catches!

Practise what you learnt on p28 and maybe you'll beat my record one day. But you'll have to be fast!

MOST FOOTBALL CROSSOVERS IN ONE MINUTE

Target to beat: 45

In 2022, I headed back to Guinness World Records HQ for a new record attempt. This time it was for crossovers, which really sap your energy. I was ready, but the nerves were still there.

Luke did such a good job timing my fourth record, I brought him with me to London! His support on the day helped me push through.

In the end I crushed it with **53** crossovers, which was nearly one per second. I was knackered, but that was my fifth world record well and truly in the bag!

For now, I'm happy with five, but it won't be long before I start coming for more . . .

What about you? Is there a record you dream of breaking? How about **'Most juggles with a tennis ball in one minute'**? (As I'm writing this book, the record is 258.)

Dream big – and if you make it to HQ, tell them I sent you! 🏉

So, Team . . .

How many new football skills have you got in your locker? Maybe it's one or two, or maybe it's ALL of them! ☺ I hope our time together in my *Footy Factory* has inspired you. Whether that's to keep trying new tricks, break world records, launch your own channel, or even just to have more fun with a football – it has been GREAT to have you here!

Ben

MY STORY

It all started with my first kick of a football when I was around 6 years old . . . I tried a training session at a local club. At first, I wanted to go home, but as soon as I got into it, I loved it!

The same year, I went to my first ever pro game – Birmingham City away at Fulham. My family supports Birmingham, so I had no choice – I had to do the same! So, it was a dream come true when I was scouted to join the Birmingham City academy at 13!

All I wanted was to play for Birmingham when I grew up, but it became obvious that other kids my age were growing a lot and I wasn't. Coaches said I was skilful, but that I would get knocked off the ball by bigger kids. I ended up being released from the club. Gutted.

I wanted to prove the coaches wrong, so I started practising skills by myself to keep sharp. I realised I loved practising alone, as I could be creative and express myself. At first, I could barely even do kick-ups, but I was addicted to improving and being able to unlock new tricks!

Everything changed when I uploaded my first YouTube video aged 11, messing around with my brother Luke. (He's got a channel now, too!) I would film myself nailing new skills and upload them to track my progress. I got hooked on this and forgot all about getting back into the academy!

Once I started breaking world records, my videos got serious attention and I was offered amazing opportunities from all over the world.

At 22 years old, I hit 1 million subscribers on YouTube. And, in my proudest moment yet, I wrote this book to inspire the next generation – you! ☺

GLOSSARY

180-DEGREE TURN: a half-circle turn

360-DEGREE TURN: a full-circle turn

ATTACK: move towards your opponents' goal

BACKHEEL: kick the ball backwards, using your heel

CHIP: a precise kick that sends the ball over an opponent's head

CROSS: passing the ball to a teammate across the pitch

CUSHION: move *with* the ball as it makes contact, to soften the impact and stop it rebounding

DEFEND: protect your goal

DRIBBLE: move forward while staying in control of the ball

EA FC: a football video game series (used to be called *FIFA*)

FIFA: a global football organisation (also the name of a football video game series – see *EA FC*)

FREESTYLE: the creative art of performing tricks and skills with a football

HEADER: using your head to send the ball in a specific direction

HIGH KNEES: running on the spot while lifting your knees towards your chest

JUGGLE: control and keep the ball in the air, using a body part

KEEPY-UPPY: another word for **JUGGLE**

LINKING SKILL: a move that helps you join one trick to another

LOFTED PASS: a long, high pass, often over the heads of opponents

NUTMEG: sending a ball through an opponent's legs

PANNA: another word for **NUTMEG**

PLANK: an exercise where you hold yourself up on straight arms with your body in a straight position, like it's a plank of wood

TEKKERS: a fun word for 'technique'!

TOP BINS: a goal scored in the top right or left corner

UEFA: a European football organisation

QUIZ ANSWERS

p17: 8147
p29: 31
p33: Neymar
p35: True
p53: 62
p59: An asteroid
p63: Accidental hand balls
p69: 39.2 km/h
p77: 18 metres
p93: The Hand of God
p97: The most times taking off and putting on a T-shirt while controlling the ball with his head (164!!!)

LOOK OUT FOR BEN'S NEW BOOK

COMING 2027!